THE LEIDEN ARATEA

Ancient Constellations in a Medieval Manuscript

Ranee Katzenstein

Emilie Savage-Smith

The J. Paul Getty Museum · Malibu, California · 1988

© 1988 The J. Paul Getty Museum
17985 Pacific Coast Highway
Malibu, California 90265

Mailing address:
P.O. Box 2112
Santa Monica, California 90406

Christopher Hudson, Head of Publications
Andrea P.A. Belloli, Editor-in-Chief
John Harris, Assistant Editor
Patrick Dooley, Design Manager
Kurt Hauser, Designer
Karen Schmidt, Production Manager
Loren Eisler, Production Coordinator

Drawing on page 16 by Leslie Thomas

Typography by U.S. Lithograph, typographers
Printed by Gardner Lithograph

All photographs courtesy University Library at Leiden.

Cover: The constellation Sagittarius from the Leiden *Aratea* (fol. 52v).

Library of Congress Cataloging-in-Publication Data

Katzenstein, Ranee.
    The Leiden Aratea, ancient constellations in a medieval
manuscript / Ranee Katzenstein, Emilie Savage-Smith.
        p.   cm.
    University Library at Leiden (Ms. Voss. lat. Q 79).
    Aratea based on the Phaenomena by the Greek poet Aratus.
    Bibliography: p.
    ISBN 0-89236-142-5.
    1. Leiden Aratea—Illustrations.   2. Illumination of books and
manuscripts. Carlovingian.   3. Constellations in art.   I. Savage
-Smith, Emilie.   II. Aratus, Solensis. Phaenomena.   III. J. Paul
Getty Museum.   IV. Title.
ND3399.L413K38   1988
091—dc19   88-39883
                                                      CIP

Contents

I

A Carolingian Masterpiece

"Our times are transformed into the civilization of Antiquity. Golden Rome is reborn and restored anew to the world!" With this boast, written in the early ninth century A.D., the poet Moduin of Autun sought to obtain the patronage of the Emperor Charlemagne (768–814). Although the product of youthful idealism and ambition, Moduin's words capture the spirit of the cultural and political revival called a *renovatio* and *reparatio* by the intellectuals at Charlemagne's court and the Carolingian Renaissance by modern scholars. Poetry and the visual arts were both enlisted in the cause of this movement, which continued throughout the reigns of Charlemagne's successors. These "sister arts," as Horace termed them, together produced one of the most representative works of the Carolingian *renovatio*, the lavishly illustrated manuscript known as the *Aratea*, now in the University Library at Leiden (Ms. Voss. lat. Q. 79).

The *Aratea* is a ninth-century copy of an astronomical and meteorological treatise based on the *Phaenomena* written by the Greek poet Aratus (circa 315–240/39 B.C.). Aratus' poem was a product of the Hellenistic Greek culture centered not at Alexandria, where scientific activity flourished, but at Athens and the Macedonian court there. Though appearing rather dry to a modern reader, it conveyed information to the general public in an easy, straightforward manner free of the literary affectations found in much of the poetry of the day. It appealed to the many followers of Stoic philosophy because of its demonstration of the providence and wisdom of the Creator: the utility of the stars to sailors and farmers is eloquently set forth by Aratus at the opening of his poem. The influence of Aratus' work was immediate and long-lasting. It served as a source for Vergil's *Georgics* and was quoted by Saint Paul. Through its many translations and revisions the poem became known in all of Europe and in the Middle East, and it informed a general audience about celestial phenomena and inspired astronomical art for well over twelve centuries. Carolingian attention to the Latin versions of the poem represents the high point of artistic interest in Aratus' work, and the Leiden *Aratea* is one of the earliest and most beautifully illustrated of the surviving manuscripts.

A small, squarish book (each page measures 22.5 x 20 cm [8⅞ by 7⅞ inches]), the Leiden *Aratea* is a parchment manuscript comprising ninety-nine leaves. Apart from

fol. 26v Cepheus

5

four folios that were already missing in 1600, the manuscript appears to be complete. The text, which runs from folio 2 through folio 97 verso, is Claudius Caesar Germanicus' Latin translation, composed in the early first century A.D., of Aratus' original Greek. This text has been supplemented by portions of a second Latin version of Aratus' poem, written by Rufius Festus Avienus in the fourth century A.D.

Thirty-nine miniatures depicting the constellations, the seasons, and the planets illustrate the *Aratea*. At least five others—representing Jupiter as a personification of the heavens, along with the sun, the moon, and two additional constellations (Virgo and Centaurus)—were originally included but are now lost. In each miniature the stars, accented with gold leaf, provide the framework for a portrait of the god, hero, animal, or object that their arrangement suggested to the ancients. Convincingly foreshortened and modeled with white highlights, each illumination presents its subject in a lively, illusionistic way.

Illusionistic techniques of this type are typical of ancient painting and, in fact, the illustrations of the Leiden *Aratea* are presumed to be copies of the miniatures made for a Late Antique manuscript, now lost, of Germanicus' treatise. Ancient art had a profound impact on Carolingian artists, who sometimes borrowed specific motifs or were, more generally, inspired by the achievements of their predecessors to portray the human form in ever more convincing and sympathetic ways. In other cases, particularly manuscripts of classical texts such as the *Aratea*, an ancient work was copied more or less directly. Although he may have modified the style of his model to conform to the norms of Carolingian painting, the medieval illuminator of the Leiden *Aratea* has assimilated to a remarkable extent the illusionistic style of the miniatures that must have formed the basis for his own work.

Other features of the Leiden *Aratea* also depend on ancient manuscript traditions. The text is written in a narrow, condensed style of script called rustic capitals (the transcription in Gothic minuscule script in the margins was added in the thirteenth century). Developed in ancient Rome, this script is based on letter forms used for inscriptions carved in stone; the shape of the serifs (the cross-line finishes of each stroke) derives from the physical process of carving in stone with a chisel. The format of the Leiden manuscript, with its squarish pages and miniatures framed as though they were independent paintings, also depends on conventions developed in antiquity.

As a faithful copy of a manuscript probably made in the mid-fourth or fifth century, the Leiden *Aratea* offers precious evidence regarding the form and content of illustrated books in the ancient world. But it is just this fidelity to its model that makes it so difficult to determine precisely where this Carolingian copy of the *Aratea* was created. The difficulty is compounded by the absence of any initial ornament or calligraphic idiosyncrasy that might help to localize the manuscript. Its subject, however, was particularly dear to members of the imperial court, and its paintings recall the miniatures in the Psalter of Emperor Lothair I (795–855), which was made shortly after 843 in Lorrain, the region along the Meuse and Rhine rivers in northeastern France where important scriptoria—at Aix-la-Chapelle, the seat of the court, and at Metz—were located. The possibility that the *Aratea* originated in this area gains support from the fact that it was almost certainly in northern France, at the monastery of Saint-Bertin at Saint-Omer, by at least the early eleventh century, when it served as a basis of another manuscript of Aratus' poem now in the Bibliothèque Municipale in Boulogne.

While the fidelity of the Leiden *Aratea* to its ancient model is striking, it is not unique. Many copies of classical or Late Antique literary works and treatises on grammar, astronomy, cosmography, medicine, geometry, and surveying were made during the ninth and tenth centuries. The most famous of these manuscripts are the illustrated ones, for instance the copies of Terence's comedies now in the Vatican Library and the Bibliothèque Nationale in Paris. It is in large part thanks to the industry of Carolingian scribes that so many of the Latin classics have been preserved. Indeed, the scholars and scribes of the Carolingian court and monastic schools were not content simply to recopy these manuscripts, but sought to improve and correct their texts. "We are concerned," states one of Charlemagne's edicts, "to restore with diligent zeal the workshops of knowledge which, through the negligence of our ancestors, have been well-nigh deserted. We invite others, by our own example, as much as lies in our power, to learn to practice the liberal arts."

Nonetheless, the Carolingian zeal for the study of the classics was not motivated by a humanist fascination with antiquity; it was rooted in what Charlemagne cited as "our duty to ensure the progress of our churches." Study of the classical past could promote this goal in two ways. Worldly knowledge better enabled Christians to comprehend theological truths. For Alcuin, the great British scholar and virtual steward of Charlemagne's cultural and educational reforms, the study of the liberal arts permitted "not only the attainment of the summit of the Holy Scriptures, but the true wisdom which is the knowledge of God." Charlemagne also depended on a revival of learning based on classical scholarship to help rid the churches in his realm of incorrect practices. It was feared, for instance, that the movable feasts of the Church year were not being celebrated on the correct days. The Carolingian fascination with astronomy, to which the Leiden *Aratea* bears such eloquent witness, was no doubt partially motivated by the aid this ancient science could offer in these important calendrical calculations. Charlemagne's interest in the subject was well known and was singled out by Einhard, his biographer, who wrote: "[Charlemagne] learned how to calculate and with great diligence and curiosity investigated the course of the stars."

In the schools that Charlemagne founded under the aegis of the bishoprics and monasteries throughout his lands, the highest standards for the production of books, both classical and liturgical, were promoted. Not only had their textual contents to be correct, but the script in which they were written had to be clear, regular, precise, and readily legible. "And do not permit your boys to corrupt [the manuscripts] in reading or writing," Charlemagne's edict of 789 enjoins. "If there is need of writing the Gospel, Psalter and Missal, let men of mature age do the writing with all diligence." It was these men, the "crowd of scribes" as Alcuin called them, who developed the forms of the Carolingian minuscule alphabet. Instead of the irregular and cramped minuscule (that is, lower-case) alphabets—cluttered with flourishes, confused with ambiguous abbreviations—that were employed in the seventh and eighth centuries, the new Carolingian script used small, neat letters that were separate and regular and thus easily intelligible. It was the perfect script with which to present the new, corrected editions of classical and Christian texts.

In addition to Charlemagne's concern for the "progress of our churches," his practical needs as a ruler underlay the revival of learning he promoted. The Church had to be staffed with an educated clergy and supplied with accurate and reliable liturgical books if it was to help secure the empire's hold over its subjects and aid in the tasks of conversion and administration that Charlemagne's sweeping conquests brought in their train. Charlemagne's concern for the instruction of the clergy and the laity must be understood, at least in part, as a conscious attempt to promote the ecclesiastical and political unity of his expanding dominions.

Finally, a political need stands behind the revival of antiquity that was such an important component of the Carolingian revival of learning. With his coronation on Christmas Day 800 as Holy Roman Emperor, Charlemagne laid claim to his succession to the Roman emperors of antiquity and, indeed, to the classical past. "If your intentions proceed," Alcuin wrote to his emperor, "a new Athens will form in Francia. What do I say, an Athens more beautiful than the ancient one, for ennobled by the teaching of Christ, ours will surpass the wisdom of the Academy."

The art and architecture that Charlemagne and his associates commissioned provided a visual affirmation of this imperial assertion. It was explicit in the paintings that adorned the imperial palace at Ingelheim, which were described by the poet Ermoldus Nigellus: "To the Imperial Conquests of the excellent city of Rome are linked the Franks and their marvellous achievements." Other works similarly evoked the imperial ambitions of the Carolingians. Charlemagne's palace chapel at Aix-la-Chapelle is patterned on the sixth-century Byzantine Emperor Justinian's foundation at San Vitale in Ravenna.

Ancient motifs, for instance egg-and-dart patterns, palmettes, and acanthus rinceaux, appear in the decorative borders of manuscripts, wall paintings, and carved reliefs. Carolingian artists adopted the techniques of classical illusionism with great sensitivity. The figures in the so-called Coronation Gospels, illuminated at Charlemagne's court in the late eighth century, are so monumental, so gracefully but believably posed, so expertly modeled by means of graduated colors and judiciously applied highlights, that they seem the products of a direct knowledge of ancient painting.

The Leiden *Aratea* expresses many of these cultural, religious, and political aspirations of the Carolingian Renaissance. Indeed, the *Aratea* was probably made for a member of the imperial court where the goals of this renaissance were defined and given lasting form. Charlemagne is known to have owned an important library, and he and his successors seem to have collected as many Late Antique manuscripts as they could (there is reason to believe that the Vergil manuscripts now in the Vatican Library once belonged to Charlemagne). They also commissioned copies of other famous Late Antique manuscripts that they could not actually acquire. The opening verses of the Leiden *Aratea*, in which Germanicus presents his work to a member of the imperial family of ancient Rome, suggest that this copy was originally made for a member of the ruling Carolingian family (perhaps Judith, the second wife of Louis the Pious [814–840]), or for someone close to the court. There is one anonymous figure whose interests coincide so closely with those addressed by the Leiden *Aratea* that it is tempting to identify him with the original owner of the manuscript. This figure—who wrote a biography of Louis the Pious which manifests so strong an interest in the stars and planets that its author is called "The Astronomer"—may have been the ninth-century antiquarian to whom we owe this masterpiece of the Carolingian Renaissance.

Ranee Katzenstein

9

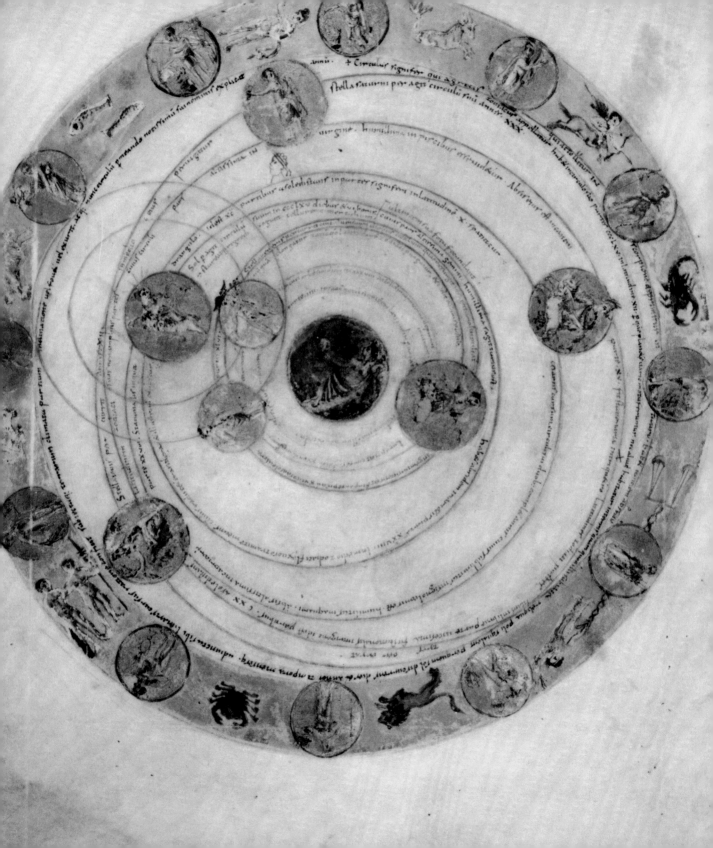

II

The Ancient Poem and Its Presentation

The Leiden manuscript is a major work of Carolingian art. But the *Aratea* is also an important document in the history of science, embodying as it does the understanding of the heavens that prevailed throughout the Western world for over a millenium. Its thousand-year-long story begins with the Greek poet Aratus.

Aratus was born around 315 B.C. in the town of Soli on the southern coast of present-day Turkey, just north of Cyprus. He wrote the poem on which the *Aratea* is based, the *Phaenomena*, at the request of the ruler of Macedonia, Antigonus Gonatas, who was renowned for the active literary circle around his court. Aratus composed hymns for Gonatas' marriage as well as other short poems, but the work for which he is most famous is this instructional poem on a scientific subject, which began a literary fashion that was to remain popular for centuries.

Consisting of 1,154 verses in Greek, the *Phaenomena* surveys the constellations and circles of the heavens and the risings and settings of the stars, concluding with a section subtitled "Omens from the Sky" that concerns weather signs. The constellations are discussed in very general terms, with no precise indications of star positions, for the primary interest of the author is the constellation imagery and the meteorological significance of the stars.

The map of the heavens which forms the basis of this poem is representative of the astronomical knowledge of classical antiquity prior to the writing of Ptolemy in the second century A.D. Ptolemy's manual of astronomy, known as the *Almagest*, was to dominate all astronomical thought until the time of Copernicus and Galileo in the sixteenth and seventeenth centuries. It is notable for the precision of its star catalogue, with magnitudes and specific coordinates assigned to each star. Such precision is not found in Aratus' poem. Some forty-eight constellations are alluded to in the poem, though these include star groups not classified as constellations by later astronomers, who considered them merely prominent star groups within larger constellations. (An example is the open star cluster of the Pleiades.)

Aratus also speaks of some star groups being always visible or, as he says, being within a circle of perpetual visibility. Since the area of the sky in which certain

fol. 93v Configuration of the Planets

11

stars are never seen to rise or set varies according to the observer's location, there have been attempts to determine at what geographical latitude the descriptions of the constellations in the poem would be valid. The most frequently suggested one is 37° or 38° north, approximately that of Athens, where Aratus worked.

According to the Roman poet and orator Cicero (106–43 B.C.), Aratus derived his entire description of the heavens not from his observations of the skies themselves but from a celestial globe on which constellation outlines were drawn. Speaking of the astronomer Eudoxus (circa 390–340 B.C.), Cicero said: "Eudoxus of Cnidos, who was a pupil of Plato's . . . marked on the globe the stars that are fixed in the sky. Many years after Eudoxus, Aratus adopted from him the entire detailed arrangement of the globe and described it in verse, not displaying any knowledge of astronomy but showing considerable poetical skill." Unfortunately, nothing remains today of the writings of Eudoxus, and nothing further is known of his celestial globe. It is certain, however, that he wrote a descriptive list of constellations, with their calendric risings and settings, which he prepared in two versions, one entitled *Phaenomena*. It is likely that Aratus employed this list of constellations when composing his poem of the same name.

The idea of constructing a physical model to represent the arrangement and movement of the stars appears to have first arisen in Greek antiquity. The stars were commonly perceived—as indeed they still are by the average person looking up at the night sky—as though attached to the inside of a hollow sphere enclosing and rotating about the earth. Consequently, the earliest attempts to represent celestial phenomena in a model were by means of a celestial globe. The earth, which was known to be spherical from early classical antiquity, was imagined at the center of the globe, while the stars were placed on the surface of the globe, so that the resulting model presented the stars as seen by an observer outside the sphere of fixed stars. On Greco-Roman celestial globes, the outlines of the constellations were drawn around the star groups so that the constellation figures seemed to be looking into the globe and to have their backs to the person using the globe. Thus, the relative positions of the stars on a celestial globe are the reverse, east to west (or right to left), of their appearance when viewed from the surface of the earth: the user of the globe would have to rely on his own imagination to place himself inside the globe, seeing the fronts of the figures instead of their backs.

The custom from Late Antiquity of drawing constellation figures, particularly the human ones, from the back, as if they are facing into a globe, is still apparent in such illustrations in the Leiden *Aratea* as Serpentarius (fol. 10v), Perseus (fol. 40v), and Orion (fol. 58v). In the case of Aquarius (fol. 48v), the artist producing the Leiden *Aratea* had the figure face the observer even though still representing the constellation as it would be on a globe, which is reversed right to left. The remaining human figures in the Leiden *Aratea* are, however, drawn as if they are in the sky looking down on the observer. (In the poem by Aratus, the descriptions of the human figures also seem to be drawn from those on a celestial globe, although a globe is never mentioned.)

Aratus referred in his poem to the movement of planets and to other celestial objects, such as the Milky Way. The planets (Mercury, Venus, Mars, Jupiter, Saturn) were called wandering stars, since they had the appearance of bright stars moving against the relatively still background of the constellations. Yet all the constellations of fixed stars appear to rotate as a whole in the course of twenty-four hours. For example, during one twenty-four-hour period, the twelve zodiacal constellations pass in front of the observer in the sequence Pisces, then Aquarius, and so forth. While appearing to rotate about the earth, their apparent motion is in reality due to the rotation of the earth on its axis—a fact unknown in antiquity. The sun, while apparently rising and setting every day, also rises each day in a slightly different position with regard to the zodiac. In this way the sun defines a path through the zodiac that is called the ecliptic.

Much attention was given in antiquity to the assigning of mythologies to the constellations, often with elaborate stories regarding the activities and relationships of the gods and the causes for their being placed in the skies. Only the most prominent stars and constellations originally drew the attention of poets and mythographers: Orion was perhaps the first constellation to which a Greek legend was attached, making him a mighty hunter with his nearby dog, Sirius. Although the images of the twelve zodiacal constellations go back to Babylonian times and are thus the oldest of the constellation outlines, they were among the last to acquire Greco-Roman legends. No myths are given by Aratus and his translators for these figures.

The myths associated with the other constellations by Aratus and his translators are limited in number; later treatises primarily concerned with astronomical lore supplied far more mythological detail. One of the most important of these was falsely ascribed to the geographer, mathematician, and literary critic Eratosthenes (circa 275–194 B.C.), who supervised the great library in Alexandria; two others were the works of a writer known as Hyginus, who composed a pair of treatises called *Fabulae* (or *Genealogiae*) and *Poetica astronomica* in the second century A.D. The latter poem presented myths associated with the constellations and was frequently illustrated. It is likely that the writings of Hyginus and that which went under the name of Eratosthenes served as sources for some of the mythological interpretations of the constellation figures made by the artist of the Leiden *Aratea* when the myth referred to is not actually to be found in Aratus or his translators.

It was through his translators that Aratus' poem became well known throughout Europe. Although its astronomical content is vague and at times inaccurate (a fact

13

frequently mentioned by commentators), it nonetheless enjoyed a great reputation throughout Late Antiquity and in the early Middle Ages.

One of the most important Latin versions of Aratus' poem was made by a writer known as Germanicus, who corrected some of the astronomical errors in the original and changed the orientation of the constellation figures from those on a globe to those in the sky. This Germanicus has generally been assumed to have been Germanicus Caesar, who was a nephew of the first-century Roman emperor Tiberius and stood in the direct line of succession. However, the poem may have been written by the Emperor Tiberius himself, who is known to have been keenly interested in astrology and mythology and was, on occasion, called Germanicus.

It is the rendering by Germanicus, whether it be Tiberius or his nephew, which forms the main part of the text of the Leiden *Aratea*. Because the Latin version by Germanicus, consisting of only 857 lines of verse, contained relatively short discussions of certain constellations, such as Gemini and Cancer, the compiler of the Leiden *Aratea* inserted portions from another Latin adaptation of Aratus' poem, one written in the fourth century A.D. by Avienus. Avienus held high office, including that of proconsul of Africa in A.D. 366. In addition to writing a number of poems, he prepared a version of the *Aratea* which considerably expanded the Greek original, resulting in 1,878 lines of verse.

In the poem by Aratus and in the Latin elaborations by Germanicus and Avienus, the twelve zodiacal constellations are described among the northern constellations. All the constellations are divided into two groups, those to the north of the ecliptic, including the zodiac, and those to the south. Most of the constellation outlines, which are merely devices for aiding in the location and recognition of a star, will be familiar to readers acquainted with modern star maps; one exception is the large southern constellation of the ship (Argo Navis), which is no longer recognized today as a constellation but has been broken up into several smaller outlines. In classical and medieval descriptions there are relatively few constellations in the southern region (one large area is completely devoid of stars), for this part of the sky remained unmapped until the geographical explorations of the sixteenth century.

In the Carolingian copy of the *Aratea* the illustrations follow in order the presentation of the material. Since few astronomical details are given in the poem regarding the constellations and their stars, there was considerable scope for the artist to interpret the descriptions. As a result, the stars, which to an astronomer are the focus of a constellation, are here treated in a somewhat cavalier manner and are sprinkled about the constellation outline with little regard to their correct positions. Even the total number of stars associated with a constellation seldom bears much similarity to the number of stars assigned in the Ptolemaic Greek star charts. It is the mythological and legendary significance of the constellation imagery that interested the illustrator, just as it did Aratus and his commentators

In the later copies of Germanicus' *Aratea* that are closely related to the Leiden *Aratea*, the illustrations begin with the figure of Jupiter, though this illustration is now missing from the Leiden manuscript. There follow thirty-six illustrations portraying the Pleiades and forty-one constellations. In the Leiden manuscript two of the original illustrations of constellations are now missing: the zodiacal constellation Virgo and the southern constellation Centaurus. Furthermore, the zodiacal constellation of Libra was probably intentionally omitted by the artist, for Libra is not mentioned by Aratus or Germanicus. (It was only after the time of Aratus that Libra's stars were distinguished by an iconography distinct from that of the scorpion preceding it.)

Of the thirty-six illustrations of constellations in this manuscript, eleven are clearly taken from diagrams derived from a celestial globe. The remaining two-thirds are oriented as they would be in the sky when viewed from earth. Consequently, it seems certain that the illustrator consulted several sources for the constellation illustrations, just as the artist occasionally drew upon an iconographical tradition of constellation representation that employed legends different from those mentioned either by Aratus or Germanicus.

The three concluding illustrations in the Leiden *Aratea* were probably derived from a different tradition than the earlier ones. The mythological personification of the five planets (fol. 80v), whose names obviously come from the names of Greek and Roman gods and goddesses, the personification of the four seasons (fol. 82v), and the twelve months which are part of the final illustration (fol. 93v)—all of these might well be related to the illustrations known to have been in a Roman state calendar made in A.D. 354 by Furius Dionysius Filocalus. (An illustrated copy of this calendar was made at the Carolingian court; although now lost, it is known through a seventeenth-century copy.) On the other hand, the planets, seasons, and the sun and moon are all mentioned in Aratus' original poem, and it is not impossible that these illustrations, along with the constellations themselves, were associated with early copies of the *Aratea* or even with the original Greek poem (though no evidence is currently available to substantiate this).

The final illustration in the Leiden *Aratea* (fol. 93v) is most certainly from a later tradition and has little direct relationship to the poem. (A modern version of it appears on page 16.) It is the earliest surviving example of a diagram illustrating the configuration of planets for one particular day. A recent historian of astronomy, after careful analysis of the diagram, has concluded that the planets are positioned as they would have been on A.D. March 28, 579.

Around the diagram is a band containing the zodiacal signs, interspersed with

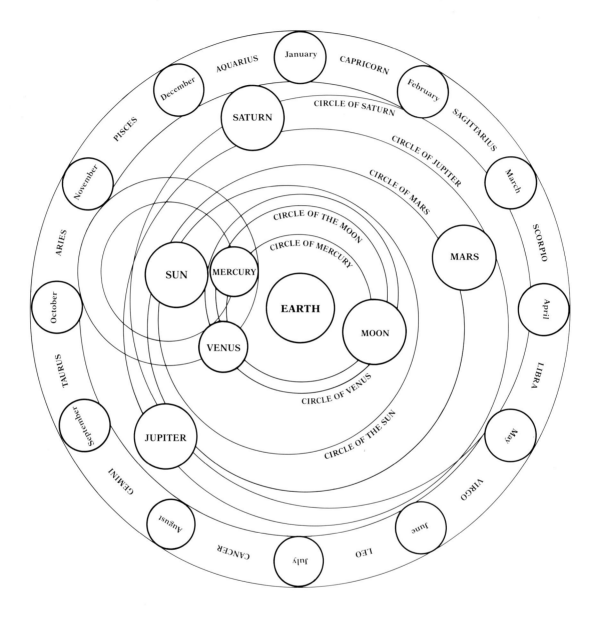

The configuration of the planets for the date A.D. *March 28, 579. Adapted from the Leiden* Aratea *(fol. 93v).*

16

medallions containing personifications of the twelve months. The sun, moon, and planets are also represented by human figures in medallions.

Written around the circular orbit of each planet are Latin quotations from the *Historia naturalis* of Pliny the Elder (A.D. 23–79). These inscriptions state each planet's point of nearest approach to (perigee) and furthest point from (apogee) the earth. They also give the exhultation of each planet, which is its position of greatest astrological influence. This astrological element, while of interest to Pliny, was generally avoided by later Latin writers of the early Middle Ages.

The circular orbits of the planets are not drawn concentrically, with the earth at the center of the diagram, but somewhat eccentrically, in order to illustrate in general terms the increase and decrease in their distance from the earth and particularly to illustrate the location relative to the zodiac of the individual planet's perigee and apogee. Near the center of the diagram, the Latin inscriptions are easily confused with the circles containing the planets, and this confusion is aggravated by the fact that the circle of Mercury crowds into and touches the moon's circle in the lower half.

While all the planets are on circles rotating about the earth at the center of the diagram, two planets (Mercury and Venus) are also placed on circles rotating about the sun, though the personifications of Mercury and Venus still stand with their feet toward earth, as do all the other planets. In producing this illustration, the unknown designer drew elements not only from Roman writers such as Pliny and from early medieval scholars, but also from a tradition of illustration in which calendars were decorated with human figures personifying the months or seasons or winds. As we have seen, at the Carolingian court a copy was drawn up of a Latin calendar originally made in A.D. 354 by Filocalus, and it is likely that this or a similar copy was the source for the representation of the twelve months by human figures placed in medallions throughout the zodiac. The addition of the month-signs contributed nothing to the astronomical significance of the total diagram. A curious error was introduced, however, by either the designer or the miniaturist producing this particular copy, for when the month-signs were drawn in the medallions, they were placed in the wrong order. They run clockwise, beginning with January at the top of the diagram, while the zodiacal signs run counterclockwise, beginning with Aries at the left of the circle. The result is that the months and the zodiacal signs are not synchronized, except at two points: January-Aquarius and July-Leo. Such an incorrect order would seem to be due to simple carelessness. This unusual diagram, then, is a Carolingian copy, at least once removed, of a sixth-century composite diagram of calendric symbols and planetary configurations corresponding to the specific date of A.D. March 28, 579.

Emilie Savage-Smith

Overleaf: Fols. 16v–17 Gemini and facing text page

AD CAPITISUBERUNT GEMINI PROLEMQ. TONANTIS

A EGRECIAM ET PROPRIO POSTREDDITA NUMINA CAELO

NALACHEDEMONIIS CUMMARS CALUISSET APHIDNIS

CASTOR ACECROPI TULIT INCREMENTIABELLI

Ad capiti suberunt gemini prolemq: tonantis
A egreciam et p̄rio post reddita numina celo
N amlache demoniis cū mars caluiss aphidnis
Castor acecropi tulit incrementia belli

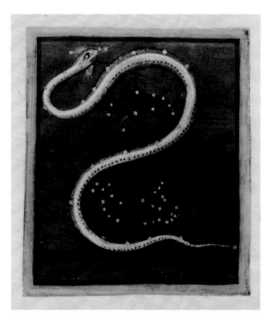

fol. 3v Ursa Major, Ursa Minor, and Draco

fol. 6v Hercules

fol. 8v Corona Borealis

fol. 10v Serpens, Serpentarius, and Scorpio

III

The Miniatures from the Leiden *Aratea*

Alcuin praised Charlemagne's love of astronomy and "knowledge of the heavenly bodies and their revolutions," an appreciation that the original owner of the Leiden *Aratea* must have shared. Although the view of the skies that modern science provides is quite different from that presented in the *Aratea*, the mythological and natural lore conveyed by its miniatures is still a source of wonder.
R.K., E.S.-S.

fol. 3v Ursa Major, Ursa Minor, and Draco
The constellations we call the Big and Little Dippers were known in antiquity as larger and smaller wagons or—more commonly—bears. According to classical mythology, when Jupiter was an infant he was sheltered by two bears named Helice and Cynosura that protected him from his father, Saturn, who devoured most of his children. Jupiter later rewarded the helpful bears by installing them in the heavens. The Greeks are said to have sailed by the larger bear because its stars are brighter, while the Phoenicians were guided (as we are today) by the Pole Star in the smaller bear. The constellation that winds between the two bears is interpreted as a serpent.

fol. 6v Hercules
Aratus calls this constellation the kneeling man: "No one knows his name or the cause of his toil." Later writers identified the man as Hercules, who won immortality by accomplishing twelve great feats known as the Labors of Hercules. The illuminator follows this later tradition and gives the figure Hercules' best-known attribute: the skin of the terrible Nemean Lion, which Hercules had strangled with his bare hands.

fol. 8v Corona Borealis
Spurned by the hero Theseus, Ariadne was consoled by Venus, who promised that she would have an immortal lover instead of the mortal one she had just lost. She was soon married to Bacchus, who gave her a gem-encrusted crown as a wedding gift. When Ariadne died, Bacchus hurled her crown into the sky, where its jewels became brighter and brighter and finally turned into stars, a lasting memorial to the god's passion for his bride.

fol. 10v Serpens, Serpentarius, and Scorpio
Asclepius, the god of healing, had dared to restore Hippolytus—the son of Theseus—to life; for this act of hubris Jupiter struck him dead with a thunderbolt. To appease Asclepius' father —none other than Apollo—Jupiter placed Asclepius in heaven. Although Aratus does not mention him, later mythographers identified the serpent-holder in this constellation with Asclepius because Asclepius' attribute was a snake. Scorpio, the eighth sign of the zodiac, was said to be the scorpion sent by Diana to kill Orion.

fol. 12v Boötes

fol. 16v Gemini

fol. 18v Cancer

fol. 20v Leo

fol. 22v Auriga

fol. 12v Boötes

This old man who, according to Germanicus, follows the bears (fol. 3v) around the heavens, may be their guardian. The brightest star in the constellation (and the fourth brightest star in the sky) is called Arcturus, which means guardian of the bear. The figure is also sometimes identified as Icarus, who shared wine with a group of shepherds. These rustics, who had never been drunk before, thought Icarus had poisoned them. They killed him, but the gods rewarded him with a place in heaven.

fol. 16v Gemini

Although Aratus did not name the twins, Avienus recognized them as Castor and Pollux. The sons of Leda and Jupiter, the valiant pair were inseparable companions. When Castor was slain dur-ing a war, Pollux begged Jupiter to allow him to exchange his own life for that of his brother. Instead, Jupiter rewarded their fraternal devotion by placing them among the stars. Castor and Pollux are shown carrying a club and a lyre, the attributes of another set of legendary twins, Amphion and Zethus, Jupiter's sons by Antiope.

fol. 18v Cancer

Hercules' second labor entailed killing the monstrous nine-headed Hydra. Each time Hercules struck off one of its heads with his club, two new ones sprang up in its place. Hercules eventually triumphed but was unable to enjoy his victory because of a crab that insisted on snapping at his foot. The hero made short work of the crab, which Juno, out of pity, adorned with stars.

fol. 20v Leo

Germanicus describes the tawny color of the lion and his shaggy mane; when the sun is in Leo, the heat of summer doubles. Later mythographers identified him as the lion that had been ravaging the valley of Nemea for many years. As his first labor, Hercules killed the Nemean Lion, and he is traditionally shown wearing its skin.

fol. 22v Auriga

Auriga is the charioteer. Germanicus suggests that he is either Erichthonis, said to be the inventor of the four-horse chariot, or Myrtilus, who betrayed King Oenomaus by substituting a wax linchpin for the metal one of his chariot wheel. As the chariot's speed increased, the wax melted and Oenomaus was thrown and killed. The celestial charioteer carries a goat and two kids, representing bright stars by which sailors can predict stormy weather.

fol. 24v Taurus

Near Auriga's (fol. 22v) feet, says Germanicus, lies the fierce bull, "his brow bearing fiery horns, his threatening head illuminated...The Hyades gleam on his brow." The Hyades are a V-shaped group of stars; the ancient Greeks and Romans believed that they indicated rainy weather when they rose with the sun. Taurus came to be identified with the white bull whose shape Jupiter assumed in order to attract and abduct Europa, the princess of Tyre.

fol. 26v Cepheus

Cepheus was the king of Ethiopia. His constellation faces that of his queen, Cassiopeia (fol. 28v), and is near that of his daughter, Andromeda (fol. 30v). Germanicus notes that Cepheus' family began with Jupiter and remarks that "the kingly nature of one's father is often an advantage."

fol. 28v Cassiopeia

Cassiopeia, the queen of Ethiopia, dared compare her beauty to that of the sea-nymphs. Indignant, these nymphs sent a sea-monster (fol. 66v) to plague her country's coast. Only the sacrifice of Cassiopeia's daughter, Andromeda (fol. 30v), would appease the nymphs. Neptune punished Cassiopeia by banishing her to a place in the sky where she hangs upside-down half the year as a lesson in humility. "Her face contorted in agony," says Germanicus, "she stretches out her hands as if bewailing abandoned Andromeda, unjustly atoning for the sin of her mother."

fol. 30v Andromeda

Andromeda was chained to a rock where she was to be devoured by the sea-monster (fol. 66v). She was spotted by Perseus (fol. 40v), who immedi-

fol. 24v Taurus

ately fell in love with her and killed the monster. As Germanicus notes, signs of Andromeda's trial remain, for "her arms are stretched...as if she were being held by the weight of a hard rock."

fol. 32v Pegasus

Out of the blood that soaked the earth when Perseus cut off Medusa's head sprang the winged horse, Pegasus. No earthly bridle could control him, but Minerva gave a celestial bridle to the hero Bellerophon, who was thereby able to tame the divine mount. Together they enjoyed many triumphs until Bellerophon, succumbing to pride and presumption, attempted to fly into heaven on his winged steed. Jupiter sent a gadfly to sting Pegasus and make him throw his rider. Thus the mythical horse entered the skies alone.

fol. 26v Cepheus

fol. 28v Cassiopeia

fol. 30v Andromeda

fol. 32v Pegasus

fol. 34v Aries

fol. 36v Triangulum

fol. 38v Pisces

fol. 40v Perseus

fol. 42v The Pleiades

fol. 34v Aries

Neither Aratus nor Germanicus identifies the ram, although later mythographers associated it with the ram that bore the Golden Fleece. Germanicus tells us that Aries moves through the longest circle in the sky. "His swiftness as he hastens to touch the distant turning post with his horns" allows him to keep up with the constellations that have a shorter distance to travel.

fol. 36v Triangulum

Germanicus calls this constellation "Deltoton" and says, "It has three sides, two equal, one shorter, but brighter" (though the illuminator has here drawn an equilateral triangle). Germanicus traces its origin to the Nile in what is perhaps an oblique reference to the river's delta. Accord-ing to Hyginus, Mercury placed this constellation—whose shape is that of the first letter of the word "Deus"—in the sky in homage to Jupiter.

fol. 38v Pisces

The twelfth sign of the zodiac is described by Germanicus as follows: "Beyond Aries lie the twin fishes, of which one stretches towards the region of the South Wind, the other seeks the region of the North Wind, that comes from Thrace.... Their movement is not free, but each is held by a chain at the tail, the chains being joined...[by] one knot."

fol. 40v Perseus

Perseus' size, says Germanicus, "is in itself sufficient evidence of his parentage: he shines so huge in all his parts, so much of the sky does the son of Jupiter occupy." Perseus wears a helmet of invisibility and a pair of winged sandals and carries an adamantine sickle, all of which he forced the Fates to give him. They helped him conquer the Gorgon Medusa, whose frightful head—with serpents for hair—he holds up in triumph.

fol. 42v The Pleiades

The Pleiades is a cluster of seven stars, six of which are easily visible. Germanicus says: "Tradition has it that there are seven [stars]...; one, however, has been taken away from this number because the eye cannot separate such small bodies." The Pleiades is a weather sign indicating the beginnings of spring and fall. The stars were identified as the seven daughters of Atlas and his consort Pleione, from whom they take their name.

fol. 44v Lyra
Aratus says that Mercury made the first lyre while still in his cradle and Germanicus notes that it is "most welcome at the banquets of the gods." A harp-like instrument, the lyre was used by the Greeks to accompany songs and recitations. It figures in a number of myths and was an attribute of Apollo and Orpheus.

fol. 46v Cygnus
Germanicus observes that while the swan's wings are bright, much of his body is without stars. He identifies the celestial swan as either the bird of Apollo or the swan whose form Jupiter assumed when he seduced Leda, the mother of Helen of Troy.

fol. 48v Aquarius
The water-carrier—the eleventh sign of the zodiac—is shown pouring out a stream of stars. Neither Aratus nor Germanicus identified him, but many later mythographers recognized him as Ganymede. The most beautiful of all mortals, Ganymede was abducted by Jupiter and taken to Mount Olympus to serve as the cupbearer of the gods. According to another tradition, he is Deucalion, who ruled the earth during the time of the Great Flood.

fol. 50v Capricorn
The tenth sign of the zodiac is represented as a sea-goat with a fish's tail. Germanicus devotes many verses to the trials of sailing in winter, the season when the sun orbits through "chill Capricorn...The brief period of daylight does not allow you to travel the distance you had hoped to.... Then comes numbness, the swift South Wind seethes over the sea, the sailors are

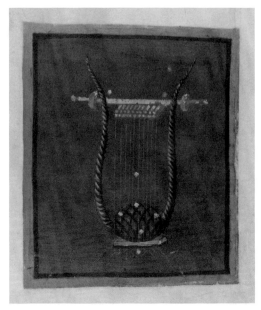

fol. 44v Lyra

slow at their tasks and trembling locks their limbs together."

fol. 52v Sagittarius
Germanicus calls this constellation "the war-waging Bow and the Beast who is pulling back the arrow in his curved bowstring." He warns mariners not to sail at night under this sign but to put up into shore in the evening. Aratus and Germanicus do not mention any legends in connection with this figure, nor even that he is a centaur, a matter of some debate in antiquity since centaurs apparently preferred not to use arrows.

fol. 46v Cygnus

fol. 48v Aquarius

fol. 50v Capricorn

fol. 52v Sagittarius

fol. 54v Aquila and Sagitta

fol. 56v Delphinus

fol. 58v Orion

fol. 60v Canis Major

fol. 62v Lepus

fol. 54v Aquila and Sagitta
Germanicus explains the combination of the eagle and arrow in this constellation as follows: it was an arrow (from Cupid's bow) that inspired Jupiter's passion for Ganymede, and it was as an eagle that Jupiter carried him off.

fol. 56v Delphinus
Germanicus gives a brief account of the events that created this constellation. Neptune's wife, Amphitrite, had run off and taken refuge with Atlas. The dolphin, "taking pity on a lover," found her and carried her back to Neptune. In gratitude for this service, the god transported the dolphin to the heavens.

fol. 58v Orion
Germanicus says of Orion: "No other constellation more accurately represents the figure of a man than the stars scattered throughout his body." According to legend, Orion attempted to seduce Pleione, the consort of Atlas, and her daughters, the Pleiades (fol. 42v). The women fled, and the gods immortalized their flight by turning pursued and pursuer alike into constellations, arranged in the sky in such a way that Orion chases his quarry forever.

fol. 60v Canis Major
According to Germanicus, the dog guards Orion (fol. 58v), who is adjacent to him in the sky. "The Greeks have given the star in [the dog's] mouth its own name, Sirius. When it lies near the sun's rays, summer blazes [hence the dog days of summer]; . . . when it rises it affects crops in two very different ways: the healthy it strengthens, but those with shrivelled foliage or feeble roots, it kills. There is no star the farmer likes more or hates more." This star, still called Sirius, is in fact the brightest star in the sky.

fol. 62v Lepus
The hare is located between the feet of Orion (fol. 58v). He is pursued by Orion's dog: "Both constellations rise and set in the sea in this way." Later mythographers said that Mercury placed the hare among the constellations because of its swiftness.

fol. 64v Argo Navis

In a time of small boats and canoes, the legendary Argo would have represented a technological revolution. This long ship, capable of holding fifty men, was built by Argos—from whom it takes its name—for Jason, the Greek hero who retrieved the Golden Fleece. Only the ship's stern appears: Germanicus reminds us that the Argo was damaged as it passed between the treacherous Symplegades (the Clashing Rocks). The stars of Argo Navis are now considered to form several constellations rather than a single one.

fol. 66v Cetus

Cetus is the monster sent by the sea-nymphs to torment the land of Cassiopeia (fol. 28v) and Cepheus (fol. 26v). As the monster rose from the sea to devour Andromeda (fol. 30v), who had been offered to it as a sacrifice, it was destroyed by the hero Perseus (fol. 40v).

fol. 68v Eridanus

It was into the river Eridanus (Italy's river Po) that Phaëthon fell when he was struck down by Jupiter's thunderbolt. Phaëthon had attempted to drive the chariot of the sun and, unequal to the task, was beginning to set the earth and the heavens on fire. Eridanus is shown as a reclining river god rather than as a coursing stream of water. This way of showing a river is a classical convention that the illuminator of the Aratea *has taken over from his antique model. The convincing illusionism of the miniature—especially the foreshortened urn and the shimmering bed of water—derives from this source as well.*

fol. 70v Piscis Austrinus

"There is a fish that swims alone, apart from

fol. 64v Argo Navis

the twin fishes" (fol. 38v). Hyginus, the first-century commentator on Aratus, identified this fish as one who rendered a kindness to the Egyptian goddess Isis. In return, she secured a place in the heavens for it and the twin fishes believed to be its offspring.

fol. 72v Ara

Germanicus describes the incense-burning altar as one of the signs that Nature has given man to protect him: "The Altar can be numbered among the sure signs of trouble at night. If the other constellations of the sky are dimmed by a covering of clouds, but the Altar is gleaming, you should then be afraid of a violent South Wind destroying the calmness of the sea."

fol. 66v Cetus

fol. 68v Eridanus

fol. 70v Piscis Austrinus

fol. 72v Ara

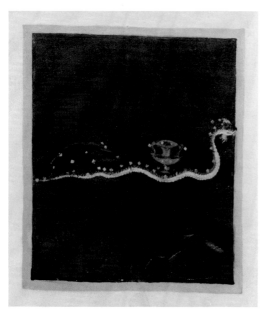

fol. 76v Hydra, Crater, and Corvus

fol. 78v Canis Minor

fol. 80v The Wandering Stars

fol. 82v The Four Seasons

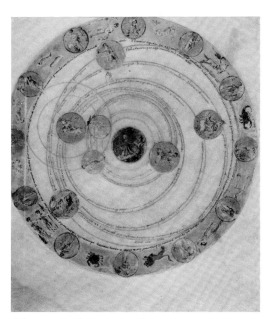

fol. 93v Configuration of the Planets

fol. 76v Hydra, Crater, and Corvus
All three constellations are linked together in a myth of Apollo. The god sent a raven, said to be one of his servants, to fetch a cup of pure water for a sacrifice. The bird, however, became distracted by a fig tree and, rather than doing the god's bidding, waited for the figs to ripen so that he could eat them. When he returned to Apollo he brought along a snake and claimed that the snake had prevented him from getting the water in the spring. The ancients believed that Apollo punished the tardy raven by making it unable to drink in springtime.

fol. 78v Canis Minor
Aratus and Germanicus mention only a single star of this constellation: Procyon, the "Fore-runner of the Dog." Its name derives from the fact that it rises before the Dog Star, Sirius. It was not until the time of Ptolemy, the second-century astronomer in Alexandria, that Procyon was described as part of a larger constellation.

fol. 80v The Wandering Stars
"There are five other celestial bodies, which travel under a different law.... They wander from the constellations they are in and change their positions.... They are often seen, rising and setting in continually changing places. Their paths are long; travelling slowly, they complete their journeys, measured in years, with difficulty." These wandering stars are of course the planets: Mercury, the messenger of the gods, with wings and caduceus; Venus, with a peacock feather (actually the attribute of Juno); Mars, the god of war, with helmet and lance; Jupiter, with scepter and fillet as the father of the gods; and Saturn, with a sickle as Father Time.

fol. 82v The Four Seasons
"Four circles which, between them, indicate the divisions of a year, cut the zodiac." The sun's passage across these circles marks the changing seasons, represented here by bust-length personifications. Spring wears a garland of flowers; Summer is crowned with wheat; Fall sports a wreath made of vine leaves; and Winter covers her head with a warm cloak.

fol. 93v Configuration of the Planets
This diagram, the earliest surviving example of its type, illustrates the configuration of the planets on a given day, in this case A.D. March 28, 579 (see above, pages 10, 15–17).

Acknowledgments

These essays have been published on the occasion of the exhibition *The Leiden* Aratea: *Ancient Constellations in a Medieval Manuscript*, held at the J. Paul Getty Museum, Malibu, from November 9 to December 31, 1988. The exhibition was made possible through the generous cooperation of the Bibliotheek der Rijksuniversiteit, Leiden, whose four-hundredth anniversary it celebrates, and was also shown at the Rijksmuseum Meermanno-Westreenianum, The Hague; the Schnütgen-Museum, Cologne; and the Pierpont Morgan Library, New York. Prof. Dr. P. F. J. Obbema, Keeper of Western Manuscripts at the University Library at Leiden, conceived the exhibition and, with Dr. Thomas Kren, Curator of Manuscripts at the J. Paul Getty Museum, arranged for the installation in Malibu. The preparation of these essays was facilitated by Anton von Euw's important study *Aratea: Sternenhimmel in Antike und Mittelalter*, published by the Schnütgen-Museum in conjunction with the exhibition there, and Dr. Ruth Kraemer's translation of von Euw's text.

References

Translations of the text of the *Aratea* are taken from D. B. Gain, *The Aratus Ascribed to Germanicus Caesar: Edited with an Introduction, Translation, and Commentary* (London, 1976). The translations of the poems by Moduin and Ermoldus Nigellus are by P. Godman, *Poetry of the Carolingian Renaissance* (Norman, Oklahoma, 1985). The quotations from Charlemagne's edicts are taken from *Translations and Reprints from the Original Sources of European History* 6 (1900), no. 5, published by the Department of History of the University of Pennsylvania. The translations from Alcuin are based upon P. Riché, *Les Carolingiens: Une famille qui fit l'Europe* (Paris, 1983). The translation from Einhard is by E. S. Firchow and E. H. Zeydel, *The Life of Charlemagne* (Coral Gables, 1972). The translation from Cicero is by G.H. Sabine and S.B. Smith, *Cicero: On the Commonwealth* (Columbus, Ohio, 1929). Analysis of the final illustration is based upon the work of Bruce Stansfield Eastwood, "Origins and Contents of the Leiden Planetary Configuration (Ms. Voss. lat. Q. 79, fol. 93v): An Artistic Schema of the Early Middle Ages," *Viator* 14 (1983), pp. 1–40.

Readers interested in further information on the subjects discussed in these essays should consult: *Aratea: ein Leitstern des abendlandischen Weltbildes* (Lucerne, 1987) [facsimile and commentary]; D. Bullough, *The Age of Charlemagne* (London and Toronto, 1965); Robert Graves, *The Greek Myths* (London, 1955); F. Mütherich and J. E. Gaehde, *Carolingian Painting* (New York, 1976); and Emilie Savage-Smith, *Islamicate Celestial Globes: Their History, Construction, and Use*, Smithsonian Studies in History and Technology, no. 46 (Washington, D.C., 1985).